About the Author

Lindsay lives at home with her husband, daughter and two dogs. She is a teacher of English as well as working in her favourite book shop. She completed her degree in English with Professional Education and Religious Studies at the University of Stirling.

Woman-19

Lindsay Tonner

Woman-19

Olympia Publishers
London

www.olympiapublishers.com
OLYMPIA PAPERBACK EDITION

A CIP catalogue record for this title is
available from the British Library.

ISBN: 978-1-80074-700-5

First Published in 2022

Olympia Publishers
Tallis House
2 Tallis Street
London
EC4Y 0AB

Printed in Great Britain

.

Dedication

To Ella, Millie, and Isla - you will rule the world.

Acknowledgements

This book couldn't have existed without my wonderful husband, Vincent, daughter, Ella, my amazing parents, Jim and Linda and the strong women that support me, Laura, Jen, Loretta and Nicola. I love you all. x

Foreword

These poems were all written during the course of a very difficult year, March 2020 – March 2021. Although they stem from my personal thoughts and feelings, I feel that many people will be able to relate. I am a woman, a mother, a wife, a daughter. I have a job, a home, a family and two lovely dogs. I have a chronic illness and disability. I live in the UK, specifically the Shetland Islands, of mainland Scotland. During these very strange times, I have felt many different emotions, you have probably felt many similar feelings. It has been a frightening time, full of uncertainty. It has been a time to rest at home with those we love, but also intensely stressful and unnerving. Even now, over a year later, when the country is starting to see a possible way out, the light at the end of the tunnel, we are still faced with so many unknowns and difficulties. So although the poems here are hugely personal to me, I hope you will find reassurance in them, I hope you will see yourself. I am just a woman. Just a parent. I am your mother, your sister, your daughter, your neighbour, your friend. I am you. My writing has given me a place to escape, hopefully you will also find that within these pages. Thank you for reading… and thank you for surviving.

Lindsay Tonner
Shetland
April 2021

1.

Will You Remember?

Will you remember?
What the world was "before?"
When we hugged and kissed, shook hands with strangers?
When we gathered in groups and sang together
as you blew out a candle on the cake we would all eat?
Will you remember the faces of your teachers? and your
friends?
or will it just be their eyes you can call to mind?
Will you remember what it was like to dance
in a darkened room, bodies tightly packed,
singing at the top of your lungs as the music drummed a
new heartbeat?
Will you remember simply walking into a shop?
and touching everything inside?
Will you remember cafes and restaurants?
Long meals and longer chats?
Setting the world to rights
over lunch with the girls?
Will you remember a time when a face mask was a beauty
treatment?
When you didn't own a cloth mask,
when the idea was strange and foreign and new?

Will you remember?
I hope you remember…
Please… remember…
but maybe it's better if you don't.

2.

Doing My Bit

I can't help but wonder,
what Rosie the Riveter would have thought
About us doing our bit,
by staying home
and watching Joe Exotic.

3.

March 2020

All of a sudden…
New vocabulary:
Self-isolation, quarantine
coronavirus, covid 19.
Money used to make the world go round,
Now fear dominates, replaces the pound.
Lock up your daughters, lock up your sons,
hide your parents before the virus comes.
The media announces a new daily death toll,
while the masses stockpile toilet roll.
Nature sends a disease to wipe out her
executioner
I'm only surprised it didn't come sooner.
We don't sing 'ring-a-roses' for this plague,
We wash our hands to 'Happy Birthday.'
Let 'the Ride of the Valkyries' play.

4.

My Greatest Achievements – A List

My greatest achievements:
The spun sunshine of your hair.
The road map of blue under whipped cream skin.
The minute mountain range of your spine.
Your sweet jungle heat breath.
The mousetrap parts that are your malleus,
hammer and incus.
The alien landscape of your tastebuds.
The mischief in your cackle.
The tiny sea-shells on your finger-tips.
Your sleep sounds, like his.
Your hand. In mine.

5.

Blissings

Bright blue een and chappet red haands.
Open taid saandels and grey paes-wisp curls.
Bony bosies and an honest, hopeful smeeg.
Da scent o Pears soap and arnica an peatsmoke
and flooer.
Ae by the stove, baking bannocks, wrapped up in
a peeny.
Waiting for night, her trows in their baeds.
Alone wi da Radio for company.
She dances wi Neil Diamond.
Ae wirkin n smiling and foo o loff n pride.
Leaving letters fae da mice.
Tae me shu will always be pink smarties an gardenias,
saffron and butterflies.
Noo shu bides abön da stars and watches ower
wis aa.

Da wind whispers спокойной ночи

6.

Mrs Right

Convince me I'm wrong,
You can't because I'm not.
I know that:
The northern lights are caused by magic.
A good cry solves most things.
Coffee is horrible.
Georgia O'Keeffe painted vulvas.
And she knew EXACTLY what she was doing.
Gin is awful.
Weeds are just flowers with a bad reputation.

And tennis balls are green.

7.

No More Land Marks

The school where we first met: closed.
The halls where we got engaged: demolished.
The church where me were married: shut.
The home where we shared a life: sold.
I lamented the loss of our landmarks.

You showed me that buildings are not our
landmarks.

The scar where she came into the world.
The crows feet and lines around your bad eye.
The glow of the northern lights.
My initial tattooed on your ring finger.
My freckles like the constellations you taught me.

8.

No More Normal

Fear.
Stalking me.
Hiding in the shadows.
This 'new normal' isn't normal at all.
You forget or try to pretend,
but it's there. Always.
Waiting to jump out and steal your breath.
Leave you gasping for air.
Tears streaming down your face.
Collecting in your mask.
Whirling. Trying to comprehend.
What is happening?!
You try to breathe. Try to understand.
Mourn yourself.
The loss of everything that came
before

and will never be again.

9.

Lockdown

The entire country slams to a halt.
But not in our little corner of the world,
not in our paradise where everything is fine.
We walk through the still, cold air, hand in hand.
Our noses turned pink and our breath turned white.
The last shining rays of winter sun are jealous of
the gold spun light in your hair.
They sky becomes more blue to rival the clarity of
your eyes.
Ice crunches beneath our feet.
Walking, keeping pace, creating a beat.
Your laughter, the joyful melody.
You can't keep your spirit still,
Outside, at one with nature, you dance like a
sprite, playing with the frost and the leaves.

10.

Creativity in Lockdown (Part 1)

Would Georgia O'Keeffe still have painted flowers?
Or just made banana bread instead?

11.

Broken

It's hard to see the silver lining
from this broken body.
At least we have our health!
but what if we don't?
Where do I fit in with my sharp edges that slice?
Every day is different because it is the same.
Blood and pain.
My bones ache. My muscles tense and twitch.
My skin itches and flakes. Red welts appear.
My skull can't contain the deep base line pounding
through my brain.
I bleed daily.

12.

Creativity in Lockdown (Part 2)

A flower without sunlight.
Will never bloom.

13.

Keeping You Close

I wish I was a better writer,
so I could bring to life how it feels,
to smell your hair and breathe you in.
I guess it's good that I can't though,
so I don't have to share you.

14.

Mother Nature

I am stronger than mountains.
More forceful than the sea.
I am a hurricane force to be reckoned with.
I am brave. I am proud. I am unshakeable and
unmovable.
But sometimes I need you to hold my hand.
To whisper in my ear that I am more powerful
than fire or ice.
To remind me that I cannot fail (but that it is ok if I
do).
To hold my broken parts together, while I apply the glue.

15.

Madam Vice President

I hope her shoulders are strong
so she can carry the weight
of the hopes and dreams
of a million little girls.

16.

Full Stop.

Aunt Flow is here…
or
Auntie Jessie.
It's my bad week, Shark week,
An unwanted subscription to Satan's waterfall.
No! It's Mother Nature's gift!
Urgh, I'm on the rag, there's a Crimson Tide.
It's The Curse! The Red Army!
That time of the month.
The painters are in, Carrie is here.
The blob, the Red Wedding, the monthly visitor.
It's Mad Cow Disease!
There's communists in the fun house!

Enough.

It's just a fucking period.

17.

Mini Me

I thought you would be more like me.
I thought you would always struggle with your
weight.
I thought you would lose yourself in books.
I thought you would be the brunette sidekick to the
blue-eyed blonde.
I thought you would favour green apples and
grapes over red.
I thought you would be confident, a leader.
I thought you would be surrounded by friends.
I thought you would be quiet and thoughtful.
I thought you would be forever unable to reach
things on the top shelf.
I thought you would be friends with the boys.
I thought you would listen to everything going on.
I thought you would eat curry and delight in food.
I thought you would dislike cats.
I thought you would love English and hate maths.

I thought you would be more like me.
But you're not...
and that's ok.

18.

Choices

All night protection.
Mini liner.
Wings, Ultra-Thin.
Basic or designer.
Disposable. Reusable. Cups. Pads. Tampon.
Endless choices for when I am "On."
Super, scented, mini, maxi.
No longer needs to feel like a nappy.
Plastic applicator, cardboard or none.
All these choices,
It's almost fun!
And yet, unlike the girls on the box,
I still can't run a marathon.

19.

New

The snow falls and everything is quiet.
Still.
The world is beautiful again.
I take the first proper breath in months.
It hangs in the air,
Before floating away.

20.

Love Song

It took me a long time to realise that
putting snow tyres on my car
is how you say
"I love you."

21.

Nearly Broken

Loving each other
is a choice we make.
Everyday.

22.

I don't believe in God,
but I talk to him regularly.
I don't believe in fate,
but I tell people 'what's for them won't go by them.'
I don't believe in karma,
but I hope she keeps receipts.
I don't believe in souls,
which is how I know he is my soul mate.
I don't believe in happy endings
but I still read fairy tales to my daughter.
I don't believe in destiny,
But I want there to be a plan.
I believe in love.
I hope that it's enough.

23.

Ella

Peerie moose,
Don't grow so fast.
They said you were pink
and I laughed.
When you were born, I went away,
I became a new person that day.
I never knew my happy every after,
would come in the middle, filled with laughter.
Play fights and power rangers, Legos and dolls.
I hold you tight, I won't let you fall.
Only eight years old and already you want to fly,
Don't grow up to soon, don't leave me behind.
We dance in the shops, we skip and we sing
but the older you get the more I'm embarrassing.
I'll always cheer you on even if you come last,
Peerie moose, don't grow so fast.

24.

Shower Thoughts

…and sometimes I wonder,
whatever happened to Neil Buchanan?

25.

FAT

2021.
Surely an enlightened time?
I read an article online…
All about how to look slimmer, thinner, not bigger.
Hide the flaws was written three times.
But to show this was a serious work,
no fluff piece or offensive dirt,
the writer employed devices like
the müller-lyer illusion, and proceeded to type
phrases such as
more massive.
My heart dropped, I felt sick.
I looked for the punchline to this poorly written
shtick.
The work of German physicist, Hermann von
Helmholtz, was cited,
and I'm sure he would have been delighted
to know that of all his wonderful
 achievements and advances
that this is how he is revered
in body shaming propaganda.

26.

Feb 14

An empty vase next to an empty decanter,
There's always next year.

27.

39 Hours

The day before yesterday I went to bed early.
Today I woke up.
I tell them I'm not well.
They tell me my blood looks fine.

28.

Lottery Ticket

Two steps forward and one step back,
A cha cha dance of death.
Every fibre of my being tells me to run
yet I am one of the lucky ones.
To protect myself from the deadly virus
I must take a chance and feel death linger
nearby.

29.

Rule Breakers

A year of isolation,
of no work or school,
no play.
We celebrate with friends and a feast!
as we always knew we would.
We never thought
it would be against the rules.

30.

2nd Shot

I walk further into the unknown
all fear is behind me
I skip along the path blindly.
there are well wishes, and hatred and envy
this is how it feels to be lucky
grateful and afraid
what has been done to me?
a dreadful experiment, a rat in a maze
Big brother ensures we behave.
this is the price of freedom

31.

Baby

Guilt. An awful, useless emotion.
I try to avoid it when I can.
Ignore it if it does come.
But now I am steeped in it.
I feel shame and horror wash over me.
The gift you bleed for,
Comes so easy to me,
that I can throw it away.
I am so sorry.

32.

Tough Enough

You take my hand and whisper,
"Pass all your pain to me."
Even if I could, I never would.
I don't know if you'd survive.
I can see it now,
an electric blue ball of lightning,
fired at you like in a video game,
electricity lighting up your back,
sparks crackling.
A vice around your ribs that you aren't aware of,
until suddenly you are.

A crushing ache for every time you try to laugh,
try to talk, try to breath.
Your hands forced into pincer shapes,
an invisible giant bending the tiny joints and
bones.
The only relief is to crack them. Snap!
It stings, like smashed pottery.
Your knees, clunking like a shopping trolley with
an out of sync wheel, reminding you with every
step, that you will never be free.
Your skin would peel, like sunburn in your mouth,

blistering and aflame like a heat gun bubbling
paint.
The soles of your feet, filled with stone and
shingle, protesting with every step and every
shoe.
The world on your Atlas shoulders, pushing you
down, compressing. The spasms traversing the
mountain range of your spine.
Every day, waking up in the Mariana Trench.
Unable to cope with the imploding pressure and
inky darkness.

You squeeze my hand.
A tear rolls down my face.

33.

It's Hard

… and it's hard.
To be who you want,
to be who she needs,
to be who they think,
to be who I can be.
Sometimes…
It's hard.

34.

Love

Your breath is heavy
you say my name like a prayer
your hands on my hips
hold me down.

35.

Harry Potter

Electricity bites at my mouth
A hidden rein jerks at my head
A sharp jolt flutters my eye.
I keep on smiling
When I'm asked
I say I feel fine
Normal
On an even keel,
And mostly I do.
The voices have gone,
The shadow people vanished
The urge and the longing have left
For now
I feel good,
How I'm supposed to.
Except for these little sparks that flutter over my face.

36.

Death of a Queen

All I have to do is open my mouth
Open my heart
Open my brain
Open my veins.
Let the words flow out
Like shards of broken glass
From between my lips.
You'll listen
You'll say thank you
Say I'm brave
Say I've made a change
Say we'll be ok.
She will look terrified
Try to clarify
All my thoughts
And feelings
And ugly
Into something with meaning
I'll come out gleaming
Shiny and new
No longer ill
Or unwell
But controlled and healing.

But I like who I am
Who I can be,
Like my crazy
My fear and my hazy
My top of the world
Conquering
Lazy perfection
My drama
My beauty
My notions and obsessions.
I don't want to open my mouth
Let any of these words come tripping out.
But I will.
For you.

37.

Just Buy a Watch

I measure time
In days
In hours
In weeks
In bottles of wine
In her height
In the before times
And the after times
In celebrations
In holidays
In disasters
In self harm scars
In the progression of her art.

38.

When I Am Gone

When I am gone,
I want you to miss me.
Not at my graveside,
Nor a church pew with solemn hymns,
Not with poetry about sad songs
I don't want you to sing in a room I am no longer in.

No, I want you to miss me as you eat an entire Victoria
sponge,
Or try to handle one too many summer bombs.
Miss me at the end of the night, as you pull the strip lashes
from your eyes,
Or when you're in a bubble bath or when your face turns to
the sky.
Miss me when the curry makes your eyes start to sweat,
Or at the karaoke as you sing Black Velvet.

39.

Tin

Cheers!
The champagne bubbles sparkle, effervesce.
Sleep now love. Rest.
Caress.
The tempest comes.
Row row row your boat.
This stream is not gentle, but we keep ourselves afloat.
Rough hands hold on to mine.
Whether the storms.
Solid as a rock.

40.

Pregnant

the word itself
pregnant

with emotion

joy
fear
shame
self-satisfaction
rage
jealousy
anxiety
apprehension
self-loathing
embarrassment
longing
anticipation
sadness
hope

so, for now
I'd rather not.

41.

Little Deaths

My tears fall like shards of ice or glass
My skin burns like salt.
I am ravaged.
I open myself up,
Kill myself off.
I die 100 times
In the name of us.

42.

I Hate You – Don't Leave Me. A Bipolar Love Story.

Don't leave me
Don't leave me
Don't leave me
I hate you; I want out.
I'm sorry.
Don't leave me
Don't leave me
Don't leave me

43.

My stomach flips,

I'm on a rollercoaster.
I know it won't end well
But I can't stop myself.

I will crash and burn
for you.

Thoughts of you burst my concentration,
Like fireworks,
Intense spark of light and then gone.
I am powerless and thoughtless,
Utterly consumed
By the flames of your desire.

44.

No Heartbeat

Why has the world not stopped turning?
The rug has been pulled,
The bottom has fallen out,
The sky has fallen in
And yet, the world keeps on turning.
Why has the world not stopped turning?

45.

Pain

Pain radiates through me.
My concrete eyelids fall.
The space in my skull is endless and full.
I spasm and writhe,
My soul aches.

46.

Bath Time

Scalding water laps on a bright red beach.
Salt burns and purifies.
The heat burns my nostrils as I inhale.
I sweat and work the knots from my shoulders.
Exhale and free my bound spirit.
Like the steam, and the Phoenix,
I rise, anew.

46.

Manic

I'm going to DO ALL THE THINGS!
I'm going to eat right, exercise, do yoga, go to bed at a
reasonable time and drink all the water.
Alphabetise my books, clean the oven and redecorate the
porch.
Lockdown? Home-school? I don't care! Yeah
I was born for this darling.
Bring it on!
We will learn outside!
Through dance and play!
We'll sing and laugh our way through time and spelling.
Strong! Fierce! Power!
But...
I know... and you know... we all know...
What goes up...

47.

Game Over

Have you seen the news?
It's all anyone ever says.
I answer no.
Why would I?
The planet is on fire,
People are fighting over a piece of life saving cloth.
Police murder innocent people.
The President spews lies.
The Prime Minister quaffs champagne as babies die of
hunger.
The world is a simulator experiment gone wrong.
The horsemen are coming.
I want to pull the plug.
Try Again.

48.

I am

I am like ice.
I am like a babbling burn.
I am like fireworks.
I am like dynamite.
I am like a duvet.
I am like a fortress.
I am like a prison.
I am like sunshine
I am like a storm.
I am like a butterfly.
I am like an arrhythmic heartbeat.
I am like you.

49.

I know you love me.
I know you always will.
Your love is endless and unconditional.
But sometimes...
I need to hear you say it.
I need to wrap myself in your scent,
Entangle my limbs with yours.
Let the tears fall where they will,
Absorbed by your skin.

50.

Trump

And now… he's gone.
He is really gone.
My heart unbreaks,
My soul rises.
I shed tears of joy. Of relief. Of hope.

51.

Blood

A serial killer documentary,
Interrupted by an adverts
Where periods have to be shown
As blue.

52.

A watermelon is just a cucumber
With a better stylist.

53.

Butterfly

Mummy, can I sleep in your bed tonight>
They're back.
The bad butterflies have come for her again.
They often come at night.
I tell her of course and hold her tight.
Smooth her hair and kiss her brow.
Try to fill her with my strength, my confidence,
Through diffusion, through osmosis, through sheer will.
I stay calm and soft but inside is sharp and crumbling.
My mighty foundation collapsing to nothing,
An almighty earthquake shatters me,
For surely, I have failed.
The bad butterflies have come again
And I know that this is only the beginning.

54.

In-Law

...and I will never forgive you,
For stealing his teeth,
For stealing his likeness,
For stealing his memories,
And calling it art.

55.

Boyfriend

You used to be the whole world,
Now you are just a series of anecdotes in my repertoire.

56.

Winter

A poem about wind and snow
No, no, no!
My toy car pirouettes on ice
Elegant and deadly.
No snowmen of children's snowball fights,
Destruction everywhere, blinding white.
The Norse gods show their wrath,
With a blind moorie, an icy blast.

57.

There Are Woman

There are woman
Who are brave and strong
Who support me
Even when I don't deserve it.

There are women
Who are funny and smart
Who love me
Even when I'm the villain.

There are women
Who are beautiful and kind
Who let me be myself
Even when I shouldn't.